Revolting
REPTILES

Revolting
REPTILES
Written by Steve Parker

Scientific Consultant Joyce Pope
Illustrated by Ann Savage

RSVP
RAINTREE
STECK-VAUGHN
PUBLISHERS
The Steck-Vaughn Company

Austin, Texas

Library of Congress Cataloging-in-Publication Data
Parker, Steve.
Revolting reptiles / written by Steve Parker.
p. cm — (Creepy creatures)
Includes bibliographical references and index.
Summary: Examines the physical characteristics, habitat, and behavior
of various reptiles, including lizards, alligators, snakes, and turtles.
ISBN 0-8114-0692-X
1. Reptiles—Juvenile literature. [1. Reptiles.] I. Title. II. Series: Parker, Steve. Creepy creatures.
QL665.P37 1994
597.9—dc20   92-43725   CIP   AC

Editor: Wendy Madgwick
Designer: Janie Louise Hunt

Color reproduction by Global Colour, Malaysia
Printed by L.E.G.O., Vicenza, Italy
1 2 3 4 5 6 7 8 9 0 LE 98 97 96 95 94 93

Contents

Revolting Reptiles

More than six thousand kinds of reptiles stalk our world. In fact, not all of them stalk. Some creep and crawl. Others slither and slide. Many swim and a few even fly! For the reptile group includes lizards, snakes, crocodiles and alligators, turtles, tortoises, and terrapins. Reptiles have scaly skin, are cold-blooded, and usually hatch from leathery shelled eggs. Delve into the mysterious world of the reptiles ...

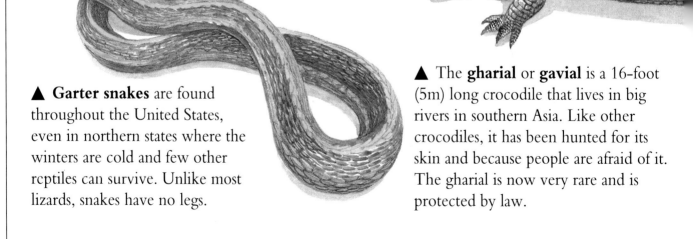

▶ The **common agama** from tropical Africa has all the typical lizard features — a slim body, four long legs with strong toes, and a long tail. Its beady eyes search for prey, and its wide mouth snaps it up.

▲ **Garter snakes** are found throughout the United States, even in northern states where the winters are cold and few other reptiles can survive. Unlike most lizards, snakes have no legs.

▲ The **gharial** or **gavial** is a 16-foot (5m) long crocodile that lives in big rivers in southern Asia. Like other crocodiles, it has been hunted for its skin and because people are afraid of it. The gharial is now very rare and is protected by law.

► **Murray River turtles** swim in rivers of southeast Australia, looking for tadpoles, frogs, and juicy water plants. They are about 12 inches (30cm) long.

▼ A survivor from the Age of Dinosaurs, the **tuatara** lives on rocky islands off New Zealand. It can reach a great age — 100 years or more. This creature looks like a lizard, but it isn't. It is the only living member of its reptile group, called Rhynchocephalia!

► About 200 million years ago, reptiles began to rule the world. Pterosaurs flew in the skies. Mosasaurs and ichthyosaurs terrorized the seas. On land strode dinosaurs like the **Tyrannosaurus** shown here. All these great reptiles died out 65 million years ago.

Loathsome Lizards

Lizards are the most successful reptiles. They live on mountains, in deserts, among trees — nearly everywhere, except for the cold poles and the open oceans. Some of the most fearsome-looking are shown here. But remember, most lizards are not harmful to people, they are only trying to stay alive, like any other animal.

▶ Beware the **Gila monster**! It is one of only two lizards with a poisonous bite. (The other is its close cousin, the Mexican beaded lizard.) Its bright warning colors tell you to keep away. Gilas can be found in Arizona and surrounding areas.

▲ Few four-legged animals can run on two legs. South American **basilisk lizards** can, the males showing off their bony "helmets" and the crests of skin on the back and tail. They can even run over water for a short distance, then they dive and swim away.

▲ Like its mammal namesake the armadillo, the **armadillo lizard** rolls into an armored ball when it is in danger. This southern African lizard grows to about 8 inches (20cm) in length and hunts spiders, insects, worms, and similar small animals.

▼ The big, powerful **caiman lizard** is named after the caiman, a type of crocodile found in the same marshy area of the Amazon. It is 4 feet (1.2m) long, and eats snails — spitting out bits of unwanted shell!

▼ The male **rhinoceros iguana** has a pointed "horn" or two on his nose. He lives in thorny scrubland on Haiti and nearby islands in the Caribbean.

▶ Covered completely in spines, the **thorny devil** ambles slowly through the desert and bush in Australia. It feeds mainly on ants.

Leaping Lizards

Lizards move in as many ways as you can think of. Many walk and run, like other four-legged creatures. Some are very fast, darting away almost before you notice them. A few race upright on their back legs. Some leap, while others paddle or swim with their tails. A few swoop and glide to safety from a tree branch or rocky cliff.

▼ The **flying dragon** of Southeast Asia is small, only about 8 inches (20cm) long. Its ribs are long and jointed and can be tilted sideways to stretch out flaps of skin that are normally folded along the body. On these two "wings," the dragon glides away from danger.

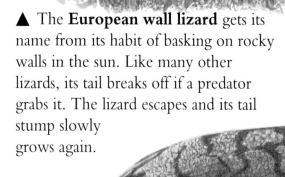

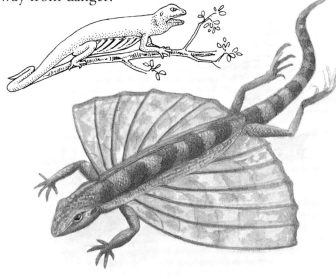

▲ The **European wall lizard** gets its name from its habit of basking on rocky walls in the sun. Like many other lizards, its tail breaks off if a predator grabs it. The lizard escapes and its tail stump slowly grows again.

▶ Walking through the Australian bush, you might be faced with a **frilled dragon** like this! When in trouble, the lizard rears up on its back legs, sticks out the frill of skin around its head, opens wide its yellow mouth, and hisses loudly! If this frightening display fails, it races away on its back legs.

frilled dragon at rest

▶ The **glass snake** looks like a snake, but it is really a lizard that has lost its legs. At 4 feet (1.2m) long, it can slither after birds, mice, and other lizards.

**frilled dragon in
defense pose**

▼ **Racerunners** hardly ever seem to stay still. They are always scurrying around, away from danger or after small animals to eat. Racerunners are the fastest lizards. They can sprint at up to 18 miles (30km) an hour.

Muscular Monitors

Monitors are the biggest and strongest lizards. There are about 30 different kinds living in Africa, Southeast Asia, and Australia. Some monitors are known as dragons or goannas. Monitors have muscular bodies and legs, and forked tongues like snakes. They eat whatever they catch — which is usually a lot!

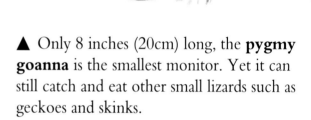

▼ The **sand monitor** is also known as the racehorse goanna because it "gallops" so fast across the Australian bush. Aboriginal people hunt it and cook its tasty flesh.

▲ Only 8 inches (20cm) long, the **pygmy goanna** is the smallest monitor. Yet it can still catch and eat other small lizards such as geckoes and skinks.

▶ The **perentie** is a huge monitor lizard of the dry Australian outback. It is 8 feet (2.5m) long. It can kill and eat a small kangaroo, yet it usually runs away and hides from people.

◀ Male monitors often stand up and battle with each other, to win females during the breeding season. **Nile monitors** stand over 3 feet (1m) tall when wrestling.

▲ A female **Nile monitor** can lay up to 60 eggs — the highest number of almost any lizard. She breaks open a termite nest and lays them inside. The termites mend the nest, so the eggs are protected. When baby monitors hatch, they scrape their way out.

▶ The **Komodo dragon** is the biggest lizard in the world. It lives on Komodo and other islands near Java. It grows to 10 feet (3m) long, and weighs 220 pounds (100kg). It can eat goats, wild pigs, and deer.

Lizards at Lunch

Most lizards are hunters. They grab and crush prey in their wide mouths, tearing off bite-sized pieces. Many are good swimmers and divers, and they chase after fish and crayfish. Some, like the chameleons, use their long tongues to capture a meal — even a fly in midair!

A chameleon sees a fly...

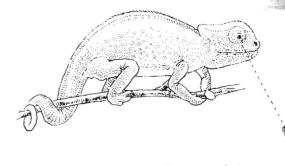

▶ **Chameleons** feed by stealth. They wait or walk incredibly slowly toward their prey. At the last moment the chameleon's long tongue shoots out, traps the prey on its sticky tip, and whisks it back into the mouth.

▲ There are about 85 types of chameleons — thin, hump-backed lizards that live mostly in trees, and mainly in Africa. They are camouflage experts. They change color to match their surroundings and wait unseen for their prey. This is **Jackson's chameleon**.

▲ The **tokay gecko** is one of the most common lizards of the gecko group. It lives in houses and other buildings, in Asia and Southeast Asia. It can climb up walls and it is a useful house guest, eating pests such as mice and cockroaches.

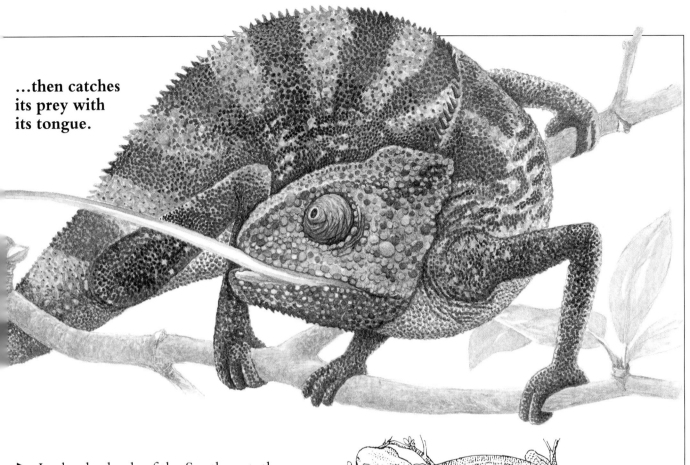

...then catches its prey with its tongue.

▶ In the dry lands of the Southwest, the **chuckwalla** hides under a rock at night. It emerges by day to feed. Unlike most other lizards, it eats plants, especially soft buds and juicy leaves.

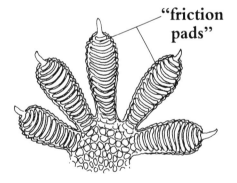

"friction pads"

▲ In addition to the usual claws, **geckoes** have feet with soles covered in tiny scales, forming "friction pads." These can grip ridges in a seemingly smooth surface. This is how geckoes climb up walls and windows, and even across ceilings.

▼ **Marine iguanas** live only on the Galapagos Islands in the Pacific Ocean. They are the only lizards that feed in the sea. They dive into the cool waters to graze on seaweeds, then bask on seashore rocks to warm up again.

Slinky Skinks

Skinks are long, thin lizards with small legs. Some have tiny, useless legs, and a few have no legs at all, so you may well mistake them for a snake. Yet they can still swim through sand, wriggle through water and undulate through the undergrowth, with great ease and speed.

▼ The Florida **sand skink** noses its way through loose sand, looking for grubs and termites. Each front leg has only one toe, and each rear leg has two toes.

▲ Through the deserts of the Middle East swims the **sandfish**, a skink that moves by paddling with its limbs, like a human swimmer. It avoids the desert heat by staying under the surface, searching for insect prey.

▶ Although it is 24 inches (61cm) long, which is very large for a skink, the **land mullet** is fast moving. In a split second it can dash into the undergrowth of its Australian rain forest home. This shiny, large-scaled skink is named after the mullet, a fish which it resembles.

◀ One of the biggest skinks, which is about 18 inches (46cm) long, the **blue-tongued skink** comes from the dry lands of Australia.

▶ The **slowworm** is not always slow. And it's not a worm, or a snake, or even a skink. It's a type of lizard called an anguid. It is also called the blindworm, but it isn't blind, either! This legless lizard lives in Europe and western Asia, and eats worms, spiders, and small insects.

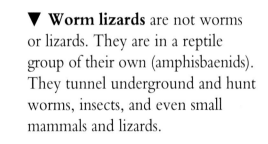

▼ **Worm lizards** are not worms or lizards. They are in a reptile group of their own (amphisbaenids). They tunnel underground and hunt worms, insects, and even small mammals and lizards.

Cruel Crocodiles...

Crocodiles are the biggest and most dreaded of all reptiles. About 22 kinds of crocodiles, alligators, caimans, and gavials make up this group of animals. For centuries they have been killed for their meat and skins, and because they attack farm animals and people. Some kinds were hunted so much that they became very rare. They are now protected by world wildlife laws.

▶ The **saltwater crocodile** is the world's biggest reptile. It grows to over 23 feet (7m) long and weighs as much as ten people. This giant crocodile lives along the coasts and river mouths of Southeast Asia and Australia.

◀ The **Chinese alligator** is one of the world's rarest creatures. There are only a few hundred left in China's Yangtze River. In ancient times people thought it was a water dragon called tou-lung.

▶ **Caimans** are crocodiles from Central and South America. They lie quietly in rivers and pools, waiting to catch animals, such as peccaries, as they come up to drink.

and Crafty Caimans

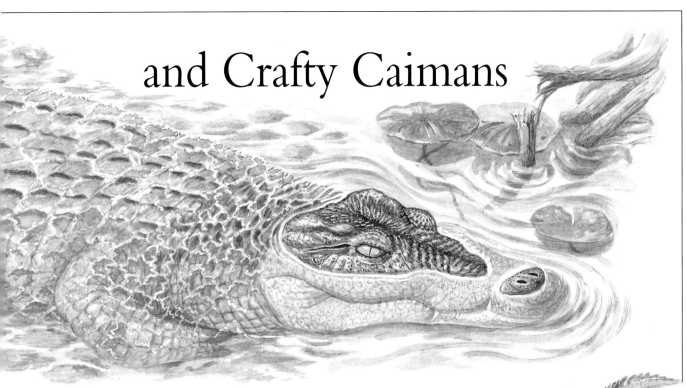

▲ Lurking low in the water, with only its eyes and nostrils showing, the **Nile crocodile** looks like an old log. When an animal comes to drink — snap! The crocodile grabs its prey, pulls it under water to drown, tears off lumps of flesh, and swallows them.

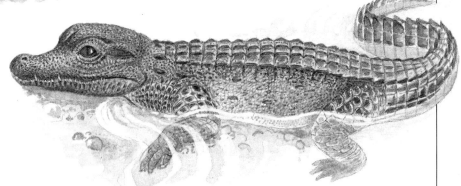

▲ The smallest crocodile is the **African dwarf crocodile**, at about 5 feet (1.5m) in length. It has a very short snout, and so it is also called the short-nosed crocodile.

◄ **Cuban crocodiles** live in just a few areas around the Caribbean island of Cuba. They eat mainly fish and turtles. But they are becoming rarer, partly because caimans (introduced into the area by people) eat their eggs and young!

Alligator Appetite

American alligators live in the southeastern United States. Many are found in Florida. In the old days they grew to over 17 feet (5m) in length, but today the biggest "gators" are around 13 feet (4m) long. A look at the life of an alligator shows how its kind have survived, almost unchanged, since dinosaurs roamed the Earth!

▼ 1. Like most reptiles, the mother **alligator** lays eggs. There are about 20 to 50, with hard shells. She makes a mound of mud, soil, and rotting vegetation near the water and lays her eggs in it. The heat released as the vegetation rots keeps the eggs warm as they develop.

▲ 2. As the baby alligators break out of their shells, they make loud "peep," "peep" sounds. The mother uncovers them and helps them escape from the mound.

▶ **American alligators** were once struggling for survival. But wildlife parks and conservation laws now protect them, so that their numbers have increased. Sometimes alligators eat pets or small farm animals. They can live for over 50 years.

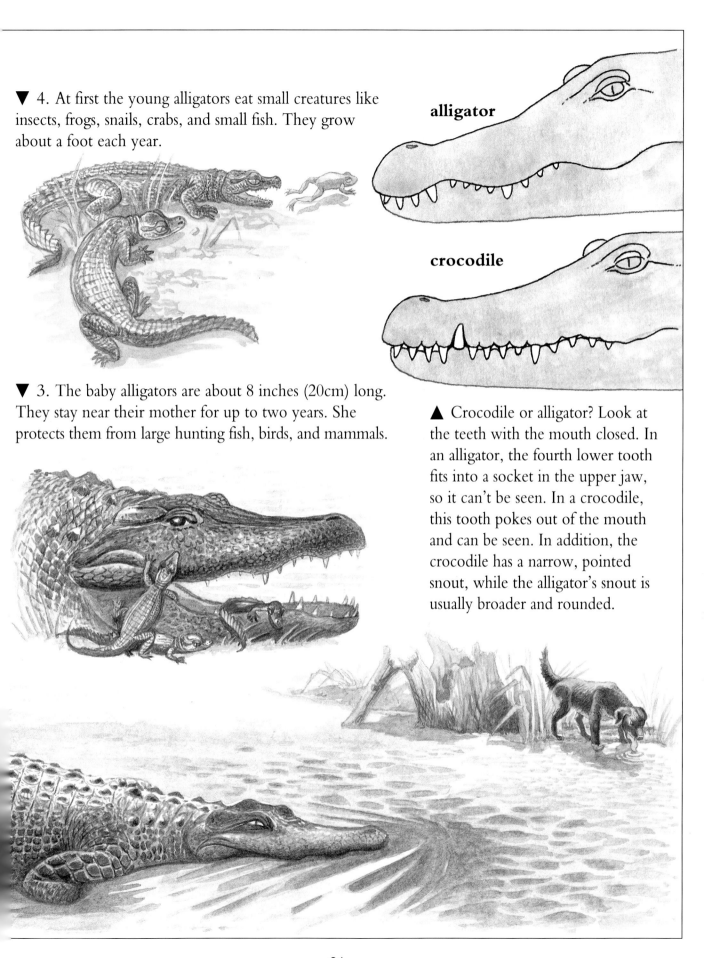

▼ 4. At first the young alligators eat small creatures like insects, frogs, snails, crabs, and small fish. They grow about a foot each year.

alligator

crocodile

▼ 3. The baby alligators are about 8 inches (20cm) long. They stay near their mother for up to two years. She protects them from large hunting fish, birds, and mammals.

▲ Crocodile or alligator? Look at the teeth with the mouth closed. In an alligator, the fourth lower tooth fits into a socket in the upper jaw, so it can't be seen. In a crocodile, this tooth pokes out of the mouth and can be seen. In addition, the crocodile has a narrow, pointed snout, while the alligator's snout is usually broader and rounded.

Slithering Snakes

Snakes have no limbs. Not even the tiniest remains of a leg or a toe can be seen. Yet they can slither at great speed, swim on the surface and dive under water, burrow into the soil, and slide effortlessly up and down tree trunks. Around the world, snakes are feared, admired, and even worshiped.

▶ All snakes are hunters. They mostly lie in wait or glide after the scent of their prey. But the **egg-eating snake** has a meal that cannot run away.

snake swallowing egg

◀ The slimmest snake must be the **vine snake** from Central America. It's longer than you are tall — but it is only as thick as your finger! It hides among the rain forest creepers and vines, and steals baby birds from their nests.

▼ Longest of all snakes is the **reticulated python**. It lives in Southeast Asia and can grow up to 30 feet (9m) in length. That's as long as eight 10-year-old children stretching out their arms and holding hands!

▼ The smallest snake is probably the **West Indian thread snake**, which is very rare. Even when fully grown, it is only 4 inches (10cm) long.

► At more than 300 pounds (135kg), this **anaconda** from the Amazon area of South America, is one of the largest snakes. This water snake is slightly shorter than the reticulated python, but it's much wider and heavier.

Squeezers and Suffocators

Some snakes poison their prey. Others simply bite and swallow them. But some snakes — the pythons and boas — have a different way of killing their prey. They coil their long body around the animal, and squeeze, and squash, and crush out the breath of life. Then they swallow their suffocated but still warm meal whole.

▶ Slightly smaller than the huge anaconda, the **boa constrictor** can tackle wild pigs and small deer. It takes up to half an hour to swallow a big catch.

▲ The **Indian python** is a typical "constrictor." This means its coils constrict its prey's breathing movements. Each time the prey gasps and breathes out, the snake tightens its grip.

▶ When it is in danger, the **Calabar python** curls into a mound of circles. Then it seems to bite the attacker. But wait — it's "biting" with its tail that's shaped and colored to look like a head. Using its tail protects the python's head, which is hidden in the coils, from a serious injury.

▲ The biggest snake in Australia, the **Australian scrub python** comes from the northwest of the country. It is large enough to swallow a small kangaroo or wallaby.

▼ **African rock pythons** grow to 27 feet (8m) long. Some say one managed to capture and swallow a leopard; another may have eaten three jackals.

▲ The **emerald tree boa**, from South America, shows the importance of body color to snakes. Its scales are patterned in bright greens so that it can hide among the rain forest leaves. But it uncoils its 6 foot (2m) length with great speed to grab passing bats, birds, and monkeys with its strong teeth.

Venomous Vipers

One lightning strike, and you feel the prick of two sharp fangs. Gradually pain and numbness spread out from the bite. You feel hot and shivery. It is hard to breathe or move, and you begin to feel dizzy. Slowly the world goes dark. This is what could happen if you were the victim of a poisonous snake. So if you see one — keep away! Luckily, most snakes are peaceable and avoid people where possible.

▼ Beware "tank-tracks" in the desert sand of Arizona, California, and Nevada. They show a **sidewinder** has passed by, throwing its body into sideways lines as it travels over the shifting sands.

▶ The **black mamba** of East Africa is not only deadly, it's also very fast. It can slither at 12 miles (19km) per hour and be out of sight before you realize it was there.

▼ A loud buzzing in the brush might not be a harmless cricket or cicada. Watch out! It could be a **diamondback rattlesnake**. This snake makes its home in southern states all the way from California to North Carolina. And it's the most dangerous snake in all of North America.

▲ **King cobras** are the longest poisonous snakes, reaching 18 feet (5.5m). When threatened, these snakes spread out the ribs and skin behind the head to make the cobra "hood." These killers eat mainly lizards and other snakes.

▼ The **bushmaster** of South America is one of the world's deadliest snakes. Its poison is fairly strong, and there is plenty of it. The snake has very long, strong fangs to inject its venom deep into its prey.

▲ The biggest and fastest poisonous snake in northern Australia is the **taipan**. Like most snakes, it usually avoids people and slithers away into the undergrowth. But if cornered, it bites several times with amazing speed.

Snakes in the Swim

Nearly all snakes can swim. Some spend almost all their lives in water. Many live in lakes, marshes, and swamps. The sea snakes, members of the cobra family, spend all their lives in the sea. They dive to catch fish and other ocean creatures, then come to the surface to breathe.

▶ The **banded sea snake** of the Indian and Pacific Oceans swims by waving its paddle-like tail. It can stay under water for two hours.

▼ The **cottonmouth** gets its name from the white inside of its mouth. It lives in southern states and rarely strays from creeks and swamps. Its strong poison kills frogs, fish, and other snakes.

venom tube

fang

venom gland

▶ The poison or venom is made in venom glands in the snake's cheeks. It flows through tubes to the snake's fangs. When the snake bites, the poison is injected through the hollow fangs into the victim.

▼ The **grass snake** is an expert swimmer. It catches frogs, fish, newts, and small birds and mammals. When threatened, it puffs up its body, falls over and plays dead, or strikes with its mouth closed.

▼ Some reptiles shed their scales a few at a time. Snakes molt or slough the whole skin at once – even the coverings of the eyes! Most snakes molt around three to five times a year.

▼ Most female **sea snakes** do not lay eggs. They give birth to several fully formed baby snakes, who can swim when they are born.

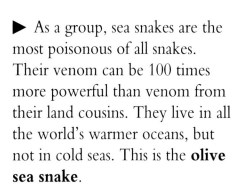

► As a group, sea snakes are the most poisonous of all snakes. Their venom can be 100 times more powerful than venom from their land cousins. They live in all the world's warmer oceans, but not in cold seas. This is the **olive sea snake**.

Turtles and Tortoises

The four main reptile groups are the crocodiles, lizards, snakes, and chelonians — the turtle group, which includes tortoises and terrapins. Turtles appeared on Earth even before the dinosaurs, over 200 million years ago. They have forsaken speed and agility for the slow life, well protected inside their thick shells.

▼ **Giant tortoises** come from the Galapagos Islands in the Pacific Ocean, and islands such as Aldabra and the Seychelles in the Indian Ocean. They grow over 4 feet (1m) long and can weigh as much as five people added together.

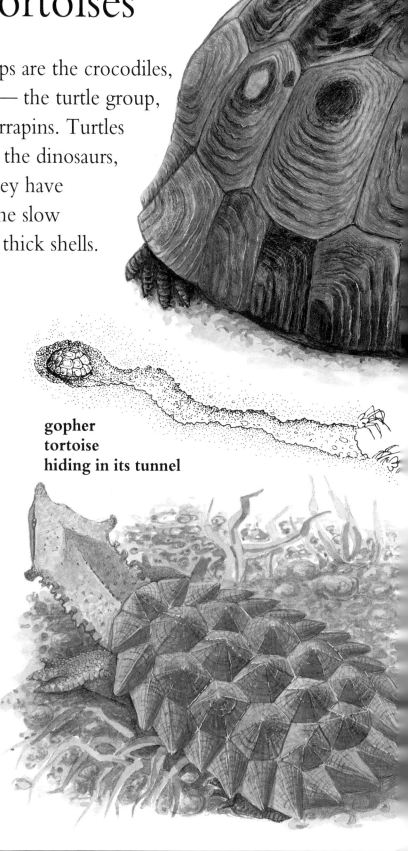

gopher tortoise hiding in its tunnel

▶ One of the strangest turtles, the **matamata** has points and ridges over its shell. It lives in South American rivers and lies in wait, ready to gulp down passing creatures.

◄ The **gopher tortoise** from Florida and surrounding states eats leaves, grass, and buds. At night it hides in a long tunnel it has dug in the soil.

▲ The **hingeback** has a folding back part on its shell, that protects its back legs. This African tortoise munches leaves and any small animals that are too slow to escape.

▼ Big and strong, the **Nile softshell turtle** grows to over 3 feet (1m) long. Like many turtles and tortoises, it is hunted by people for food.

▲ The **alligator snapping turtle** lives in parts of the United States and lies on the bottom of a deep lake or river. It opens its mouth to show a pink, worm-like part that wriggles invitingly. Fish come to look, and snap! They are gone.

Traveling Turtles

There are seven kinds of sea turtles. They are the biggest and most traveled of the turtle group, swimming thousands of miles each year. In the past they were hunted for their delicious flesh. Today they are protected by world wildlife laws.

▼ Female **sea turtles** come on the shore to lay their eggs in sandy beaches. They dig a hole, lay about 100 pale, leathery-shelled eggs, and cover them with sand. Sadly, hotels and resorts have taken over many turtle-nesting beaches.

▶ Baby **sea turtles** hatch out after several weeks. They run to the sea, but many are eaten by gulls, snakes, lizards, and other hunters.

▶ **Green turtles** feed mainly on seaweeds. Their flesh is very tasty and was used to make turtle soup. They grow up to 4 feet (1.2m) long.

▲ The **Atlantic ridley** is the smallest sea turtle, with a shell only 30 inches (76cm) long. Its strong jaws can crunch up crabs, shrimps, sea snails, and fish.

▲ The **leatherback** is massive — over 8 feet (2.5m) long, and weighing almost 2,000 pounds (900kg). It roams the world's oceans, protected by a tough shell that feels like stiff rubber. Its main food is jellyfish.

▶ Once the **hawksbill** was hunted for its shell. It was turned into tortoiseshell for combs, ornaments, and other items. Today this is against the law.

Glossary

Amphisbaenids A small group of unfamiliar reptiles, sometimes called "worm-lizards." They look like big worms or small snakes.

Breeding season The time of year when male and female animals of the same kind come together to mate, and raise young.

Camouflage Colored and patterned to merge and blend in with the surroundings.

Chelonia The reptile group that includes turtles, sea turtles, terrapins, and tortoises.

Cold-blooded An animal that cannot control its body heat. Cold-blooded animals get heat from their surroundings. On hot days they are warm and active. On cold days they are cool and move around very little.

Conservation In nature, the act of saving wild places, and the animals and plants that live there, and making sure they are not damaged in the future.

Constrictor A type of snake that winds its coils around its prey and then squeezes tight, squashing the breath out, and suffocating the victim.

Defense pose Body position and behavior designed to make an animal look big and fearsome, to scare away rivals and predators.

Dragon In legend, a lizardlike reptile with wings that breathes fire and guards treasure. In real life, the name "dragon" is given to some types of lizards, like the frilled dragon of Australia.

Eggs Small rounded objects, laid by a female, from which the young animals grow. Reptile eggs are usually pale, with tough leathery shells.

Fangs Extra-long, extra-sharp teeth, usually at the front of the mouth. Snakes use them to bite and inject their poison.

Molt When an animal casts off its body covering and grows a replacement. A snake wriggles out of its old set of skin-and-scales.

Predator An animal that hunts other creatures, called prey, for food.

Prey A creature that is hunted for food by other animals called predators.

Reptile A cold-blooded animal with a backbone and scaly skin, that lays eggs with leathery shells. (A few reptiles, such as certain snakes, give birth to fully formed babies; some lay hard-shelled eggs.)

Ribs Long, slim bones that wrap around the chest. In a snake, they wrap around the whole long body.

Scales The platelike coverings in the skin of a reptile. Scales are made of a horny material, light but hard, like your fingernails.

Tortoiseshell The polished, colored, patterned, plastic-like substance once obtained from the shells of turtles and tortoises, especially the hawksbill. It was used to make combs, hairclips, ornaments, and similar items.

Venom glands Body parts that make venom, or poison. In a snake, they are usually in the rear part of the head.

Warning colors Bright colors and patterns that make an animal easy to see. They warn that the animal is dangerous or tastes bad.

Index

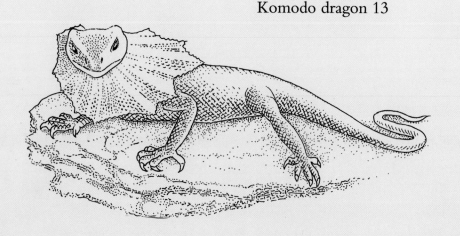

A TEMPLAR BOOK

Devised and produced by The Templar Company plc
Pippbrook Mill, London Road, Dorking,
Surrey RH4 1JE, Great Britain

PHOTOGRAPHIC CREDITS
t = top, b = bottom, l = left, r = right
All photographs are from Frank Lane Picture Agency (FLPA)
page 8 Stephen Dalton/NHPA/FLPA; *page 9* L. Robinson/FLPA;
page 12 L. Robinson/FLPA; *page 13* C. Jeske/Silvestris/FLPA;
page 15 Eric and David Hosking/FLPA; *page 17* K.G. Preston-Mafham/
Premaphotos Wildlife/FLPA; *page 22* Eric and David Hosking/FLPA;
page 23 M. Wendler/Silvestris/FLPA; *page 24* Eric and David Hosking/
FLPA; *page 25* T. Allan/FLPA; *page 26* A. Bannister/NHPA/FLPA;
page 27 M. Ranjit/FLPA; *page 29* S. Summerhayes/Biophotos/FLPA;
page 30 J. Karmali/FLPA; *page 33* T. and P. Gardner/FLPA